A SPINE OF 33 MYSTERIES FOR THE NEW CULTURE

Soror XNC

Baby Lyon Press

AZ

ISBN 978-1-257-84583-5

www.thenewculture.com

www.tmol360.com

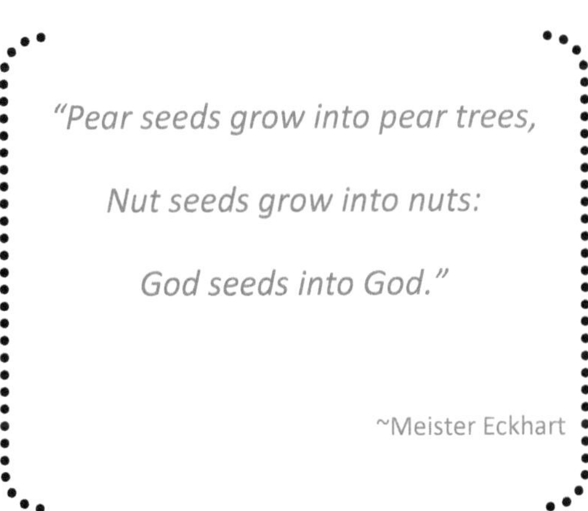

"Pear seeds grow into pear trees,

Nut seeds grow into nuts:

God seeds into God."

~Meister Eckhart

CONTENTS

INTRODUCTION

We are the "God Seeds". The time has come to act like it. It is up to us to reclaim our civilization by consciously refashioning our lives.

This material can serve all awakening seeds. Applied as a whole to the systems of civilization and *coordinated to a greater locational time system* it can reflect what we call UMMA – an archetype of the best existence obtainable and proto-image of cultural ideals. UMMA is the non-tangible, Prime Example of a Wisdom-based Utopia. UMMA is the goal.

Consider that culture is a machine. At present, the machine is geared to produce and value monetary gains. But the culture can be intentionally retooled through our own Power of choice, for the purpose of cultivating a new era of enlightenment.

Toward this end, I provide you this document; a spine of 33 permutations of consciousness, each representing a renewed articulation of the social machine. These permutations were originally received with the title of *The Hinge ME*, or collectively, *the MES*. They are referred to as "The Arts of Civilization" as they cooperatively convey Civilization's best possible expression as a study, skill and technique requiring thought, passion and perspective. They are also referred to as a "Mystical Science" as they allow for the natural Order of the Ages to be implemented on Earth by way of a specific formulary arrangement of underlying construct.

The MES have existed on Earth before, in previous eras and specifically interpreted to befit their location in time and place. In present day, they might be conceived of as something like the algorithms of an operating system for society, executed as a whole or in parts, enabling movement, process and the output of function.

I received this spine across 260 days, commencing from the first minute of December 17th, 2002 to be punctuated on the last minute of September 2nd, 2003 and contained within a larger Work called *Liber Ouranos* or The Bark of Heaven. The grantor of this Work, having a Lion's face, a Serpent's Wisdom, and the Peacock's mantle, is called by many names, but by me, Shemyaza.

Now, with the creation of this document, I am putting forth the 33 MES as an independent device to serve The Movement of LIFE and the emergent New Culture.

Soror XNC

6.28.2008

ME 0 – THERE IS A SEED; LOVE

GNOSIS

SYMBOLIC TONGUE: A Date Palm, tall and straight, bares abundant clusters of ripe date fruit, dripping with aegis nectar around which clusters of bees swarm. This Palm, like the celestial pole, a reminder of Center, and surrounded by clusters of stars that swarm like buzzing, golden bees transmitting their immortal, astral dew.

ACTION: Self-Realization. Liberty. Every man and woman, a Star; every Star, a constellation; together, all, we are a collection of flames, an inferno of knowledge.

Just as bees make honey as a byproduct of their natural, sustaining activities, so is the supreme function of civilization to "make Light" out from the unique and specific nectar of its own unfolding Star-Beings.

ME 1 – THERE IS AN ENDLESS CIRCUMFRANCE ENCIRCLING ALL

AWARENESS

SYMBOLIC TONGUE: A beautiful, everlasting jewel, not to be found in polished stones but made in a Herculean feat of Nature, formed deep in the bowels of adversity through unbelievable pressure and stress, seemingly unbecoming or insignificant parts vulcanized together into something new – a stunning, seamless whole said to gleam with the reflection of every flame.

ACTION: Oneness, and absolute restoration of the prevailing consciousness thereto.

Restoring our State of Union through Awareness (within, with others, and within the greater orchestra of Life) is a similar feat. This is why the on-going process of (re-)Union (into greater wholes) is known as the "Great Work".

ME 2 – THERE IS A TRUE DIAMOND RING OF UNION

WISDOM

SYMBOLIC TONGUE: Here lies a symbol in motion: One circle of completion becomes two polarities of the same ONE Thing. Then, the duality of intersecting circles and each again derives polarity. Here is the Quaternity, born. Calculate its portions by the point of Reason at Heart of the center. In this supreme unity, the indestructible matrix of the diamond is found – a Magick Child. For it is the fetus of the Union, even as a Human fetus is derived wholly of its original four divisions.

ACTION: Join; gather whole parts into greater wholes. Four points are used to quantify all things; each point can alter in quality. Each thing is calculated by its Knowing, its Motion (or Silence), its Will (or Force) and its Intensity (or Potency).

There are four inseparable elements of which the entire Universe is formed. There are four fundamental directions of manifestation that together allow for the truth to be discerned.

ME 3 – THERE IS A PATTERN AND A LIMIT

UNDERSTANDING

SYMBOLIC TONGUE: In a civilized land, the populous are the offspring of their cradle's *nature* and the collective *nurture* of the prevailing consciousness. A populous, born from the intersection of society with the Divine. Their Mother; their defined medium of existence. Their Father; their exemplar. Together, in the Chi Rho Cross.

ACTION: Direction is everything. Pick one. That is your core of Reason and your goal. Now define your core with four Qualities – a thought, emotion, energy and form – so as to grant your Reason preeminent existence.

The Ultimate Frontier is subjective; a culture can take aim at or idealize any direction. Where the Ultimate Frontier is conceived of as expression of a Divine Consciousness, Awareness is paramount. A culture of Awareness deliberately extracts a specific environment of tone, temperament, personality, function and so forth. It is an intentional Way of Life designed to induce consciousness and bring Life to the Divine Ideal.

ME 4 – THERE IS POTENCY IN HIGHWARD CHARACTER

ORIENTEERING

SYMBOLIC TONGUE: A pyramid, upright and crowned in illumination; providence shining favor over a well-ordered plan. The world mountain, abode to the Divine, coordinating the direction of Above with the directions of below.

ACTION: Direction is everything. Center yourself. Temper your temper. Take aim and stay the course. Push back your horizons. Ascend in altitude. Whirl with the Stars.

Once upon a time there was a cradle of Life which was known to visibly model the forces and laws which structured the Universe for those who were patient enough to gain understanding. From these heroine and exemplars came the great astro-empires. When an illumined character champions over adversity to stay the course of Universal Grace, Humanity will once again live lives Divinely expressed.

ME 5 – THERE IS STRENGTH IN DYNAMIC SYNTHESIS

STRENGTH

SYMBOLIC TONGUE: From action issues release of Life and Light. From the five-fold hand of action issues the release of Life and Light. Action, arranged like speech is arranged (to convey Intention) is a wand. From the hand, grasping the wand, issues the release of Life and Light – a thunderbolt, a vitalizing spiral force, enriching and fertilizing the medium of growth.

ACTION: Break things down into ordered parts. Build them back together into a New Union, refined to better convey Intention. This is the process called Strength.

Synthesis is the essential science for any desiring Union within and with others. The Science of Synthesis is inherent to achieving the Ultimate Frontier of Union with the Divine Consciousness.

ME 6 – THERE IS SYNERGY IN COMBINED INTENTION

BEAUTY

SYMBOLIC TONGUE: Beauty, rescued from her sleep, begets an Arcadian existence.

ACTION: All are creative, whether or not it is realized. Assure your creations bear witness to your true state of Awareness. Live in beauty with others.

Truly united effort achieves a grand efficiency and wondrous freedom that could never be enjoyed by individuals working alone.

ME 7 – THERE ARE WORDS OF HONOR TO BREED WORLDS OF GRACE

ABUNDANCE

SYMBOLIC TONGUE: Victory! The enduring forest! One lush body, a multiplicity of dynamic flora and fauna in an ever-changing container of natural systems and structures.

ACTION: Assure actions bear witness to your true state of Awareness. Orchestrate your behavior to serve the greatest good.

Life is woven together as a tapestry is woven together. The integrity of the fabric relies on the integrity of the interdependent threads.

ME 8 – THERE IS A WAY TO ARRANGE ALL PARTS SO AS TO HEAL THE WHOLE

ILLUMINATION

SYMBOLIC TONGUE: A healing wand of miracles; the fire-quickened mind. Glowing; a lamp to stay the course. A wand where the Solar and Lunar fluid intertwine; the great, transformative agent. The letters of the Universal language spelled out into the perfect medium; Stars in the cosmic sea.

ACTION: Superior organization derives superior function derives superior form. An illuminated mind can expect miracles. Collect and organize all parts with intelligence

Awaken and correlate the Whole presence within; gather and collect the scattered or disorganized bits outside. Make them one body, a Star.

ME 9 – THERE IS STABILITY IN DIVERSITY

THE FOUNDATION

SYMBOLIC TONGUE: Letters spilled in every shade appear white. The building blocks tumbled from words; in every shade. White Limestone, well-chiseled.

ACTION: Create, recognize and use diversity. There is bounty, affluence and a manner of insurance for any body/environment which maintains a full-spectrum of qualities. Increasing our base of Knowledge preserves us.

Differences in contrast become a stumbling block. All unique qualities are composite to the full-spectrum of Human expression – be it related to the individual or the group.

ME 10 – THERE IS A WORLD TO CREATE

THE KINGDOM OF ELEMENTS

SYMBOLIC TONGUE: Vocalize! Stand upright in the center, aligned by the Laws which borne you. Aligned to the Six-Directions! An amalgam of Power, Character and Intention; a seed of Knowledge and Energy fully grown.

ACTION: Let All Have a Voice! An individual's pursuit of creative Self-Mastery is a core necessity to the Social Whole.

Replace the Human-Doing Experiment with the Human-Being Experience. When Humans are in a state of conscious Being, stellar Actualities unfold and Become.

ME 11 – THERE IS A WAY TO SERVE HUMANITY

VIRGO

SYMBOLIC TONGUE: That which Neutralizes and Vitalizes. Bathing. The renewed fire of the renewed day. Feast and Fast.

ACTION: Mastery over personal and collective action. Arranging action on behalf of neutrality and in accord to a natural model.

Action determines character. Actions congruent to spiritual ideals purges the limitations of overly personalized realities and dissolves the chatter of lower identifications. This uplifts and vitalizes.

ME 12 – THERE IS A TRUE COMMITMENT TO HONOR

LIBRA

SYMBOLIC TONGUE: That which tallies ones works and draws like to like. The balance. The yoke of Union. Yoga.

ACTION: Mastery over personal responsibility to a greater whole.

Because the inherent nature of Humanity is collective, there is an inherent need deep within the Human heart to join together with others in combined action. Working together with another, or with a multitude of others, balances and refines the character and elevates energetic dignity.

ME 13 – THERE ARE INVISIBLE FORCES DISCHARGING THROUGH THE STREAMS OF LIFE

SCORPIO

SYMBOLIC TONGUE: That which releases and transforms. Sexual orgasm. Transition. Alchemy. Lingam-yoni. The wand and vessel.

ACTION: Mastery over magnetism and power. Develop informed relationships with energy, energy exchange and wielding personal power. Ritual.

Knowledge is Power, literally. This Power is known through the yearnings and impulses of Desire. Even as a magnet, an individual is compelled along by Desire – forming, releasing or altogether resisting the energetic connections and bonds which generate all motion and transformation.

ME 14 – THERE IS STRENGTH IN BENDING

SAGITTARIUS

SYMBOLIC TONGUE: That which initiates with trails. The iris. The rainbow. The bow of the Archer. The strength of the arch.

ACTION: Mastery of aim and attainment. Look beyond division to seek a connecting source. Growth always; in every adversity, growth.

When White Light penetrates a curve it is bent and appears as a spectrum of color, each so apparently distinct from the other, yet each merely a variation of the same ONE Thing. At the same time, this division, tempered and recombined, provides the insight necessary for the ONE Thing to be restored.

ME 15 – THERE IS IMPERFECT UNDERSTANDING WHEN WE SEE THINGS ABSENT OF THEIR COMPLETION

CAPRICORN

SYMBOLIC TONGUE: That which can confuse with appearances. The eye. The orb of the world. The circumference of the horizon.

ACTION: Mastery of appearances. Honor the unseen portion. Account for holistic Being. Discard shadows of doubt. Create the path. Humans and all aspects of this world are Divine. Accept the true inheritance.

Humanities' physical eyes are limited in their scope and therefore perceive limitation by their very nature. The view is even circumscribed by the limits of the horizon; while the world continues beyond. When eyes are left to determine the world, they invert it.

ME 16 – THERE IS AN UPLIFTING FORCE THAT DRAWS ALL CONSCIOUSNESS TOGETHER INTO AN UNBROKEN STREAM

AQUARIUS

SYMBOLIC TONGUE: That which reveals a Universal Hope. The Star. Electricity. Thunder and Lightning.

ACTION: Mastery of Forethought. Experimentation, Quest, Research. Thought genesis. Epiphany. Ecstatic excitement. Meditation.

In moments of concentration, visualization, meditation, revelation, ecstasy, epiphany, etc., there is an open channel to a greater state of consciousness that, like lightening to soil, can fertilize the mind with new information.

ME 17 – THERE IS A PLACE WHERE PERSONAL REALITY AND COSMIC ACTUALITY MEET AS ONE

PISCES

SYMBOLIC TONGUE: That which organizes the greater body. Cerebellum and medulla oblongata of the Human brain. Reflection. Sleep. Vehicles of change. Mushrooms.

ACTION: Mastery of corporeal reality. Enlightenment. Theofication. Ascension. Spiritual practice for conscious participation in subconscious activity.

The lower personality merely spins within the cycles of time until Awakening to the Truth that by consciously participating in the Great Work of Theofication there is Liberty.

ME 18 – THERE IS INSIGHT IN DESIRE

ARIES

SYMBOLIC TONGUE: That which reasons on behalf of desire. Windows. Visions. Sexual longing. The ankh.

ACTION: Mastery of personality. Personal Survey. Self-Mastery. Personal contribution to the whole.

The greater good is Served whenever and wherever an individual can follow ambition and aspiration, purpose and potential. Whole, healthy, well-energized Humans know what it is to have a contributing niche in the greater body.

ME 19 – THERE IS INTUITION IN HEEDING THE DELICATE HARMONY OF THE STREAMS OF LIFE

TAURUS

SYMBOLIC TONGUE: That which hears and joins. A nail, link or ring.

ACTION: Mastery of possession and permanence. Linking the personal consciousness with the collective consciousness. Stewardship. Dynamic possession. Personal and collective economy.

The Streams of Life must flow without blockage and stagnation. No thing is permanent. No thing is without change. Yet there is enduring abundance when affairs are managed on behalf of conscious harmony with Life.

ME 20 – THERE IS DIVISION THAT MUST BE MADE WHOLE

GEMINI

SYMBOLIC TONGUE: That which has knowledge of good and evil. A sword. Twins or lovers. Fruits (of effort, of the natural world, et al).

ACTION: Mastery of division. Bonds, marriage contracts. Pursuits which transfer things or ideas (ie transportation, communication). Dialogue.

It is necessary to account for the apparent divisions and dualities of the ONE Thing. Bridge all gaps with discernment.

ME 21 – THERE IS AN INCOMING POWER THAT MUST BE SUITABLY LODGED

CANCER

SYMBOLIC TONGUE: That which conquers illusions of material shells. Bees and their hive. The senses. A fence. The globe of living worlds.

ACTION: Mastery of motion while in a material shell. Mastery over illusions, especially of permanence. A powerful abode.

The descent of celestial forces into matter is the cause of all manifestation. Thus, true also is that the individual, physical body is the abode of a cosmic presence.

ME 22 – THERE IS STRENGTH IN PURPOSE

LEO

SYMBOLIC TONGUE: That which awakens through control. The lion. The serpent-power. Reverberation.

ACTION: Mastery of self-articulation.

Modes of self-expression that align to the cosmic presence are potent with synergy. Modes of self-expression that align to Higher Will and provide an instrument to carry forward its force.

ME 23 – THERE IS A QUALITY IN BECOMING[1] THAT IS KNOWN THROUGH CAUSALITY

MARS

SYMBOLIC TONGUE: The sacred energy of the base is marked by the sacred bone of the spine. It requires release.

ACTION: Appropriate action. Equal exchange. The most beneficial outcome for all affected. Positive economy.

For every action there will follow a second action caused by the first. And this reaction will be either pleasant or unpleasant in its ultimate effect, in full accord to the vibrational quality of its cause.

[1] Externalized energy expression. All things.

ME 24 – THERE IS A QUALITY IN BECOMING THAT IS KNOWN THROUGH RECIPROCITY

MOON

SYMBOLIC TONGUE: The abode of the Life essence gives forth the codes of replication. It requires clarity.

ACTION: Appropriate Relationships. Unity. Integration. Abstinence from violence, force and coercion.

What is given is ultimately what is returned.

ME 25 – THERE IS A QUALITY IN CONSCIOUS BEING THAT IS IDENTIFYING

SATURN

SYMBOLIC TONGUE: The personal appetite designed for a city of jewels. It requires a boundary.

ACTION: Appropriate perspective. Ego containment. Highward by design. Character.

All things share an interconnected existence. Nothing is independent. The individual identity is a wave in an ocean of waves, even as each wave crests with its own potential.

ME 26 – THERE IS A QUALITY IN BECOMING THAT IS KNOWN THROUGH BALANCE

VENUS

SYMBOLIC TONGUE: The affective soul is triumphant when unstruck by extremes. It requires an opening of the Heart.

ACTION: Appropriate effort. Service. Compassion. Magnetic attraction. Love.

Cultivate a boundless Heart toward All Life. Pervade the world with the free-flowing abundance of Liberty for All. There is always a door between the two-sides.

ME 27 – THERE IS A QUALITY IN CONSCIOUS BEING THAT IS DIRECTING

SUN

SYMBOLIC TONGUE: The center is Will, around which all else turns, at every level of existence. It requires revival.

ACTION: Appropriate Intention. Emanation. Creation. A wand. Responsibility.

Consciousness requires intentional forethought of the whole to counter-balance free reign of the individual center. As consciousness increases, so too does responsibility increase within the cosmic orchestra.

ME 28 – THERE IS A QUALITY IN BECOMING THAT IS KNOWN THROUGH ILLUMINATION

MERCURY

SYMBOLIC TONGUE: The House of Mind well administrated. It requires admission.

ACTION: Appropriate Mentality. Truth discrimination. Justice. Non-judgment.

Truth is a birthright. To receive the full lot of the inheritance, be a witness to Self. Judge no thing.

ME 29 – THERE IS A QUALITY IN CONSCIOUS BEING THAT IS LIBERATING

JUPITER

SYMBOLIC TONGUE: There is a crown; it blooms like a flower in the presence of the Divine. It requires expansion.

ACTION: Appropriate Mindfulness. Benevolence. Grace. Universality. Leadership that surrenders to providence. The Highest Greatest Awareness.

Conscious Awareness achieves the height of material expression and Ascension from the same.

ME 30 – THERE IS ABSOLUTE BECOMING

NEPTUNE

SYMBOLIC TONGUE: A golden objective collectively rendered through Great Work. Immortal Life.

ACTION: Initiates ennoblement. Mysticism. Spirituality.

As the limits of present understanding are transcended and thereby expand, mater becomes increasingly responsive to the intent of immortal Being. The obligation of consciousness is becoming aware.

ME 31 – THERE IS WISDOM

URANUS

SYMBOLIC TONGUE: A field of the blessed, ceaselessly fertile, within which lives all ideal forms. Light.

ACTION: Initiates restoration. The medium of transmission. The space between. The pattern and system.

When things do not adapt and evolve, they end. When vibrational motion slows, Life-progress retreats proportionately. Light is the great informer.

ME 32 – THERE IS ABSOLUTE BEING

PLUTO

SYMBOLIC TONGUE: The eye of a storm holds a great secret that only experience can reveal. Love.

ACTION: Initiates Union. Reason. Gnosis.

Within Absolute Being, all extremes are neutralized. The reason to its whole expression is known.

www.ingramcontent.com/pod-product-compliance
Ingram Content Group UK Ltd.
Pitfield, Milton Keynes, MK11 3LW, UK
UKHW041903190726
13854UKWH00003B/1063